THE SILENT

The Sisters Who Only Spoke to

Each Other

By

Brian Lakers

Table of Contents

June and Jennifer Gibbons were born just like every other child with nothing unusual surrounding their birth. Their parents however noticed something very strange about the girls when they reached the age where they should have been talking but refused to talk and only to be mute to everybody. Their parents also realized that the girls were far behind their peers in regard to language skills and also unusually inseparable. The two girls seemed to have a private language that only they could understand.

In the year 1947, the family relocated to Haverfordwest, Wales from England. On getting to their new base, the two girls became inseparable.

John Ress, a medic however noticed something very strange about the girls which then prompted him to report to a child psychiatrist. Even with the therapy given to the girls, nothing seems to work for the girls to talk. They refused to talk so much that their language became more idiosyncratic which later on twisted into idioglossia - private language

4

understood only by the twins themselves and their younger sister. Discover the reason behind their keeping mute and what eventually happened to the silent sister.

Chapter One
Jennifer and June

June and Jennifer were born on April 4, 1963 at the military hospital in Aden, Yemen, where their father Aubrey had been deployed. Not long after the girls got to the age while they should be talking, their parents Gloria and Aubrey Gibbons noticed something very strange about them. Their parents realized their girls will not talk and were also away far behind their peers in regard to language skills, but they were also unusually inseparable, and the two girls seemed to have a private language that only they could understand.

The Gibbons family later relocated to England and then, in 1974, they moved to Haverfordwest, Wales. On getting to their new base, the twin sisters became inseparable. They would however discovered that they were the only black children in their community which made them to be subjected to being bullied and ostracized. The two girls being bullied was also as a result of the way the girls talk. The girls spoke very fast and had little grasp of English, making it difficult for anyone to understand them. The bullying got so bad that this proved to be traumatic for the twins, eventually leading them to being dismissed early each day so that they might avoid bullying. By the time the girls became teenager, their language had become unintelligible to anyone else. They also refused to communicate with anyone and also refused to read or write in school.

The girls language became known as what is known as idiosyncratic which eventually twisted into idioglossia – a private language adapted and understood only by the twins themselves and their younger sister, Rose. The girls language was later discovered to be a mix of Barbadian slang and English. At one point, the girls wouldn't speak to anyone even their parents but themselves and their sister.

Chapter Two
Isolation and Therapy

In the year 1974, John Rees a medic noticed something very strange about the girls while administering a yearly school-sanctioned health check. The medic noticed that the twins were unusually non-reactive to being vaccinated describing their behavior as "doll-like". The medic noticed that June and Jennifer showed no emotion when getting the injection which prompted the doctor to notify their headmaster before contacting a child psychiatrist.

The medic after observing this quickly alerted the school's headmaster. The headmaster however brushed him off stating that the girls were just naturally quiet. Rees who was not satisfied with this reply then decided to notify a child psychologist. The psychologist on seeing the two girls and examining them, immediately insisted that the girls be enrolled in therapy. Even with the therapy given to June and Jennifer, the two girls refused to speak to anyone else.

In February of 1977, anther speech therapist named Ann Treharne, met with the two girls. The two girls however refused to communicate in Treharne's presence, the two consented to having their dialogues recorded if left alone. The therapist however noticed that one of the girls, June wished to talk to her but Jennifer compelled her not to do so. Treharne later said: "Jennifer sat there with an expressionless gaze, but I felt her power. The thought entered my mind that June was possessed by her twin." It was later suggested that the two girls should be sent to different boarding schools with the hope that they will be forced to communicate with other people wherever they find themselves. And on this, at age 14, the girls were sent to separate boarding schools as part of the treatment, in an hope their self-isolation will break, and that they will be back in normal life. Even with this, the two girls didn't perk up until they were reunited. Their separation later revealed that the two girls were emotionally and psychologically bound to each other so much that they could neither live together nor apart. They were inseparable. It was during this period that it was even discovered that the two girls have this ritual of deciding which one of them would wake first, which one would breathe first, and the other wasn't allowed to breathe until the first one breathed. This was discovered when one of them was rigid and remain in a fixed position.

On being separated and far away from each other, June and Jennifer Gibbons instead withdrew entirely into themselves and became almost catatonic. At one point during their separation, it took two people to get June out of bed, after which she was simply propped against a wall, her body "stiff and heavy as a corpse." Bizarrely, the other twin would be in an identical pose, despite the fact that the girls had no way to communicate with each other or coordinate such an event. It was immediately clear that the experiment was a failure. On this, the twins were reunited. On being reunited with each other, the twins hewed even more tightly to one another and then became more withdrawn from the rest of the world so much that they no even longer spoke to their parents, except for communicating by writing letters.

Chapter Three
Mental House

As inseparable as they were, the girls have their dark side. They do have excessively violent fights that involved throttling, scratching, or otherwise harming one another. In one incident, June made an attempt to kill Jennifer by drowning her. In one of the entry discovered in Jennifer's diary, she wrote:

"We have become fatal enemies in each other's eyes. We feel the irritating deadly rays come out of our bodies, stinging each other's skin. I say to myself, can I get rid of my own shadow, impossible or not possible? Without my shadow, would I die? Without my shadow, would I gain life, be free or left to die? Without my shadow, which identify with a face of misery, deception, murder.' Due to their affinity for writing, police also later on discovered a large stack of diaries, poems, essays and short stories, some written about crime.

They had such a talent for storytelling that June's book – titled Pepsi Cola Addict – about a student being seduced by a teacher was self-published. The sisters were also known to always retreat back in their room spending their time playing with dolls and creating elaborate fantasies that they would sometimes record and share with their younger sister Rose — by this time, Rose was the only recipient of communication in the family. One of the girls later revealed in her diary that: "We had a ritual. We'd kneel down by the bed and ask God to forgive our sins. We'd open the Bible and start chanting from it and pray like mad. We'd pray to Him not to let us hurt our family by ignoring them, to give us strength to talk to our mother, our father. We couldn't do it. Hard it was. Too hard."

When they were 16 years old, the twins took a mail-order writing course, and began pooling together their small financial assets to publish their stories. The themes of their self-published novel were as strange and worrisome as their behavior.

After the printing of their book, the silent twins became bored with simply writing and longed to experience the world firsthand. By the time they were 18, June and Jennifer Gibbons had started experimenting with drugs and alcohol and began committing petty crimes.

They began having flings with boys, and committing crimes. They also got engaged with common crimes such as shoplifting and burglary. The girls took another turn to their crime when they decided to commit arson setting fire to a tractor store. A few months later, they did the same thing to a technical college which turned into a devastating fire incident within minutes—it was this crime that dragged them in Broadmoor Hospital, a high-security mental health hospital, with a reputation for handling the criminally insane in 1981.

Here, June would go into a state of catatonia and attempt to commit suicide, while Jennifer lashed out violently at a nurse. one would starve while the other would eat her fill, and then they would reverse their roles. They displayed an uncanny ability to know what the other was feeling or doing at any particular time.

The girls' 11-year stay in Broadmoor was both unusual and unethical at some Point—June later blamed their lengthy stay at Broadmoor on their speech issues:

She later said: "Juvenile delinquents get two years in prison...We got 11 years of hell because we didn't speak... We lost hope, really. I wrote a letter to the Queen, asking her to get us out. But we were trapped

Chapter Four

The Secret Agreement

An in-depth look at the mysterious lives of June and Jennifer Gibbons being hospitalized at Broadmoor Hospital did not prove easy for June and Jennifer Gibbons. The high-security mental health facility was not as lenient about the girls' lifestyle as their school and family had been. Instead of letting them retreat into their own world, the doctors at Broadmoor began treating the silent twins with high doses of antipsychotic medicines, which caused blurred vision for Jennifer.

For nearly 12 years, the girls lived at the hospital, and their only respite was found in filling page after page in diary after diary. June later summarized their stay at Broadmoor: "We got twelve years of hell, because we didn't speak. We had to work hard to get out. We went to the doctor. We said, 'Look, they wanted us to talk, we're talking now.' He said, 'You're not getting out. You're going to be here for thirty years.' We lost hope, really." Finally, in March of 1993, arrangements were made for the twins to be moved to a lower-security clinic in Wales.

On their way to the new facility, Jennifer rested her head on June's shoulder and said, "At long last we're out." She then slipped into some sort of coma.

However, upon arrival at the facility, something strange happened to Jennifer. Doctors noticed he was unresponsive. She had seemingly drifted off during the trip and wouldn't wake up. On this, she was taken to a nearby hospital not until they reached Wales that any doctor intervened, and by then it was too late. At 6:15 she was pronounced dead as a result of sudden inflammation of the heart. Jennifer Gibbons was just 29 years old when she died.

While the official cause of death was believed to be the major swelling around her heart, Jennifer Gibbons' death still largely remains a mystery. There was no evidence of poison in her system or anything else unusual.

After her sister's death, June wrote in her diary, "Today my beloved twin sister Jennifer died. She is dead. Her heart stopped beating. She will never recognize me. Mom and Dad came to see her body. I kissed her stone-coloured face. I went hysterical with grief."

Jennifer's untimely death had a shocking effect on June: She suddenly began speaking to everyone as if she had been doing so her whole life.

June Gibbons was later released from the hospital shortly after, and by all accounts began living a fairly normal life. When asked why she and her sister had committed themselves to being silent for nearly 30 years of their lives, June simply replied, "We made a pact. We said we weren't going to speak to anybody. We stopped talking altogether — only us two, in our bedroom upstairs."

END

Printed in Great Britain
by Amazon

14322339R00020